Middle School Vocabulary Challenge

Written by Linda Schwartz

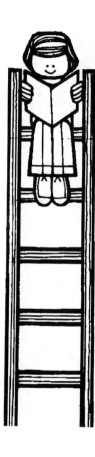

The Learning Works

Editorial production and page design by
Clark Editorial & Design

Cover illustration by *Kelly Kennedy*

The purchase of this book entitles the individual teacher to reproduce copies for use in the classroom.

The reproduction of any part for an entire school system or for commercial use is strictly prohibited.

No form of this work may be reproduced, transmitted, or recorded without written permission from the publisher.

Contents

Introduction

Middle School Vocabulary Challenge is a collection of fun and easy-to-use vocabulary-building activities designed especially for the middle school classroom. *Middle School Vocabulary Challenge* is divided into six high-interest areas:

- Vocabulary Warm-Ups
- Prefixes and Suffixes
- Synonyms and Antonyms
- Analogies
- Words for the Week
- Fun With Words

For your convenience, a master list has been provided on pages 120–127 featuring the vocabulary words presented in the book and the page numbers on which they appear.

Middle School Vocabulary Challenge contains instant activities that can be used in a wide variety of ways, such as:

- class openers
- "word-of-the-day" challenges
- supplements to class topics
- learning center activities
- extra credit
- homework assignments
- bonus points on unit exams
- study tools for standardized tests

Reproduce the activities, write them on the board as daily word brain teasers, use them to make a bulletin board game, or transfer them to overhead projector transparencies. The uses are endless!

4

Ideas for Using *Middle School Vocabulary Challenge*

- Mount the "Vocabulary Warm-Ups" on large index cards and place them at a vocabulary center in a file box. Have students use the cards as they complete their class assignments. Answers can be written on the backs of the index cards to make the exercises self-correcting.

- After completing the "Analogies" section, have students work with a partner to create their own analogies for their classmates to solve. Ask them to create analogies using antonyms, synonyms, parts to whole, animal groups and offspring, etc.

- Give each of your classes the "Words for the Week" as a Monday quiz and see how many perfect scores each class gets. Keep track of the weekly winners and see which class is the champion for the semester with the most perfect scores.

- Reproduce the "Word List" on pages 120–127 and send the list home with each student so parents can see new words their students are learning. The word list also makes an excellent guide for students to use while preparing for standardized tests throughout the year.

- Using the ideas presented in "Fun With Words," have students work in small groups of four to five to create their own vocabulary activities using themes such as sports, food, weather, and occupations.

Using the Answer Key

No collection of activities would be complete without a collection of answers. In this book, the answer key appears at the back of the book on pages 128–136. To make answers easier to find, they have been listed by page number and keyed by letter to a particular position on the page. Thus, answer **a** is for the word (or activity) on the upper left side of the page, answer **b** is for the word on the upper right side of the page, answer **c** is for the word on the lower left of the page, and answer **d** is for the word on the lower right side of the page. (See diagram.)

a	**b**
c	**d**

Middle School Vocabulary Challenge is a fun-filled book you and your middle-school students will enjoy all year long!

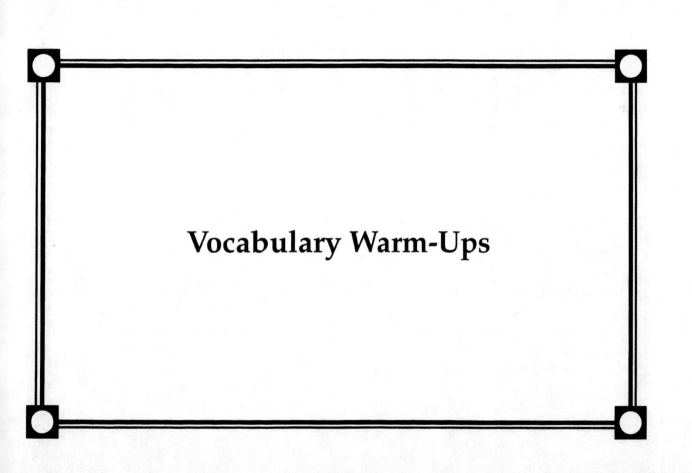

Vocabulary Warm-Ups

In each group of words, select the best definition for the word in bold.

urbane
- a. rural
- b. raucous; loud
- c. urgent
- d. polished
- e. evasive

impede
- a. hinder
- b. stampede
- c. exaggerate
- d. falsify
- e. announce

assimilate
- a. to confuse
- b. to polish
- c. to absorb
- d. to present or give
- e. to predict

usurp
- a. take over with force
- b. make a squealing sound
- c. to free from entanglements
- d. emphasize
- e. understand

In each group of words, select the best definition for the word in bold.

paradox
- a. waiver
- b. contradiction
- c. document
- d. composition
- e. paradise

transitory
- a. unnecessary
- b. portable
- c. brief
- d. irritating
- e. reciprocal

rancid
- a. rotten
- b. feeble
- c. juicy
- d. solitary
- e. rapid

fortitude
- a. honesty
- b. courage
- c. praise
- d. vigor
- e. fascination

In each group of words, select the best definition for the word in bold.

adroit
  a. useful
  b. courteous
  c. hasty
  d. thrifty
  e. skillful

fiasco
  a. complete failure
  b. debate
  c. figurine
  d. maze
  e. culmination

facetious
  a. phony; false
  b. sarcastic; joking
  c. tardy
  d. serious
  e. knowledgeable

concise
  a. sharp
  b. curious
  c. timely
  d. hidden
  e. brief

In each group of words, select the best definition for the word in bold.

reprimand
   a. to repeat
   b. to scold
   c. to praise
   d. to conceal
   e. to grieve

plethora
   a. troops
   b. abundance
   c. disease
   d. poverty
   e. confusion

novice
   a. regulation
   b. priest
   c. journey
   d. beginner
   e. thief

mettle
   a. courage
   b. award
   c. dunce
   d. illness
   e. rebellion

In each group of words, select the best definition for the word in bold.

validate
    a. to approve; confirm
    b. to tremble
    c. to forgive
    d. to misbehave
    e. to abuse; slander

precipice
    a. cliff
    b. particle
    c. parasite
    d. punishment
    e. rebellion

wizened
    a. intelligent
    b. pointed
    c. shriveled
    d. deadly
    e. enraged

treacherous
    a. clear
    b. sensuous
    c. tremulous
    d. cowardly
    e. dangerous

In each group of words, select the best definition for the word in bold.

magnanimous
   a. gentle
   b. magnified
   c. generous
   d. all-powerful
   e. warlike; quarrelsome

obliterate
   a. to pass on to; hand down
   b. to lie
   c. to contain
   d. to examine
   e. to wipe out completely

pacify
   a. to continue
   b. to disturb
   c. to appease
   d. to spread
   e. to humiliate

trepidation
   a. fear
   b. grief
   c. intense pain
   d. bondage
   e. revenge

In each group of words, select the best definition for the word in bold.

frivolous
- a. humorous
- b. trivial
- c. stubborn
- d. tactless
- e. talkative

astute
- a. stark
- b. ancient
- c. slender
- d. shrewd
- e. innocent

tumult
- a. attack
- b. earthquake
- c. vault
- d. rebuke
- e. commotion

concede
- a. hide
- b. admit
- c. attach
- d. view
- e. recede

In each group of words, select the best definition for the word in bold.

frugal
  a. healthy
  b. fattening
  c. thrifty
  d. wild
  e. hesitant

thwart
  a. cancel
  b. block
  c. struggle
  d. reduce
  e. propose

divulge
  a. divide
  b. promise
  c. reveal
  d. involve
  e. irritate

acrimonious
  a. gloomy
  b. despicable
  c. flavorful
  d. bitter in speech or manner
  e. unpredictable; changeable

In each group of words, select the best definition for the word in bold.

gamut
  a. rival
  b. glove
  c. fake
  d. sample
  e. range

opulent
  a. overweight
  b. greedy
  c. luxurious
  d. brilliant
  e. opposite

redolent
  a. reluctant
  b. vigorous
  c. clumsy
  d. odorous
  e. boring

dubious
  a. doubtful
  b. eminent
  c. durable
  d. delinquent
  e. defensive

In each group of words, select the best definition for the word in bold.

capitulate
   a. to strike
   b. to surrender
   c. to criticize
   d. to support
   e. to intimidate

disperse
   a. to scatter
   b. to doubt
   c. to deny
   d. to rotate or spin
   e. to project

flamboyant
   a. hot
   b. flexible
   c. feverish
   d. showy
   e. serious

volatile
   a. vague
   b. practical; useful
   c. explosive; unstable
   d. unresponsive
   e. unreasonable

In each group of words, select the best definition for the word in bold.

posthumous
a. plausible
b. underground
c. hidden
d. original; the first of a kind
e. occurring after death

dowdy
a. shabby; old-fashioned
b. droll
c. mystical
d. distorted
e. grim; ghastly

jaunt
a. jinx
b. short trip
c. small group
d. fake; imposter
e. narrow stream

loiter
a. to litter
b. to become weak or feeble
c. to hang around; linger
d. to toss overboard
e. to agree

In each group of words, select the best definition for the word in bold.

agitate
    a. to infect
    b. to overcome
    c. to stir up; shake
    d. to fill to capacity
    e. to loathe

credence
    a. belief
    b. culmination
    c. fear
    d. force
    e. corruption

obfuscate
    a. erase
    b. steal
    c. demolish; destroy
    d. alternate
    e. confuse; make obscure

voracious
    a. outrageous
    b. visual
    c. eager to absorb or consume
    d. vivid
    e. loud

In each group of words, select the best definition for the word in bold.

cordial
- a. devious
- b. cowardly
- c. coarse
- d. friendly
- e. narrow

replicate
- a. to reproduce or copy
- b. to anticipate
- c. to bid
- d. to honor
- e. to fear

ludicrous
- a. heavy
- b. ridiculous
- c. affable
- d. luscious
- e. intelligent

tawdry
- a. cheap; showy
- b. light brown
- c. wise
- d. loyal
- e. transparent

In each group of words, select the best definition for the word in bold.

docile
    a. apparent
    b. obedient
    c. sullen
    d. belligerent
    e. fragrant

plutocracy
    a. liberty
    b. delegation
    c. successor
    d. ruled by the masses
    e. government by the wealthy

travesty
    a. journey
    b. mockery
    c. pathway
    d. treatise
    e. trauma

dearth
    a. dedication
    b. death
    c. talent
    d. conclusion
    e. scarcity

In each group of words, select the best definition for the word in bold.

eschew
- a. reclaim
- b. scream; yell
- c. avoid
- d. swallow
- e. allow

periphery
- a. discussion
- b. broad expanse
- c. embellishment
- d. outer edge or boundary
- e. growing year-round

salient
- a. saturated
- b. similar
- c. prominent; noticeable
- d. smooth
- e. equal

dormant
- a. steady
- b. inactive
- c. determined
- d. harsh
- e. excessive

In each group of words, select the best definition for the word in bold.

tenuous
    a. nervous
    b. every ten years
    c. flimsy
    d. tender
    e. useless

domicile
    a. residence
    b. calmness
    c. sympathy
    d. art of respect
    e. dweller

pilfer
    a. to lunge
    b. to deny
    c. to delay
    d. to steal in small quantities
    e. to influence

garish
    a. spooky; frightening
    b. futile
    c. tarnished
    d. grateful
    e. flashy; gaudy

In each group of words, select the best definition for the word in bold.

contrive
- a. assemble
- b. expose
- c. make public
- d. distract
- e. plan; devise

feasible
- a. difficult
- b. possible
- c. fancy
- d. false
- e. delicious

sporadic
- a. allergic
- b. precise
- c. occasional
- d. jerky
- e. specific

buffoon
- a. clown
- b. sail
- c. harpoon
- d. musical instrument
- e. fish

Prefixes and Suffixes

A **prefix** is a letter or sequence of letters attached
to the beginning of a word, base, or phrase.

A **suffix** is a letter or sequence of letters that has a specific definition
and may be added to the end of a word or base to change its meaning.

The prefixes **ab-** and **abs-** mean *from* or *away*. Define each word and use it in a sentence.

  abdicate
  abrade
  abscond
  absolve

The prefixes **contra-**, **contro-**, and **counter-** mean *against*. Define each word and use it in a sentence.

  contradict
  contraband
  controversy
  countermand

The prefix **hyper-** means *over* or *too much*. Define each word and use it in a sentence.

  hyperpyrexia
  hyperbole
  hypertension
  hyperpnea

The prefix **omni-** means *all*. Define each word and use it in a sentence.

  omnipotent
  omnivorous
  omniscient
  omnifarious

The prefix **inter-** means *between* or *among*. Define each word and use it in a sentence.

    intercede
    intercoastal
    interpret
    intermittent

The prefix **mal-** means *bad, wrongful,* or *ill*. Define each word and use it in a sentence.

    malaise
    maladroit
    malign
    malfunction

The prefix **quad-** means *four*. Define each word and use it in a sentence.

    quadrant
    quadrille
    quadruplet
    quadrennial

The prefix **hypo-** means *under* or *too little*. Define each word and use it in a sentence.

    hypothermia
    hypopnea
    hypogenous
    hypodermic

The prefix **tri-** means *three* or *triple*. Define each word and use it in a sentence.

> trident
> trilogy
> tripod
> trisect

The prefix **post-** means *after*. Define each word and use it in a sentence.

> postpone
> postmortem
> postscript
> postoperative

The prefix **mono-** means *one* or *single*. Define each word and use it in a sentence.

> monologue
> monopoly
> monotonous
> monocle

The prefix **circum-** means *around*. Define each word and use it in a sentence.

> circumnavigate
> circumscribe
> circumference
> circumlunar

For each box, name the prefix that can be combined correctly with all four words.

act	vision
tend	test
claim	long
plain	gram
frost	deed
light	stall
plane	dent
rail	side

For each box, name the prefix that can be combined correctly with all four words.

mission	spell
mend	print
pound	place
bat	manage
jury	violent
son	believer
form	malignant
cent	verbal

For each box, name the prefix that can be combined correctly with all four words.

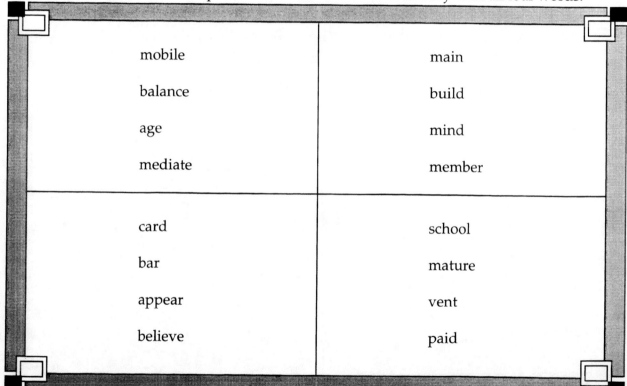

mobile	main
balance	build
age	mind
mediate	member

card	school
bar	mature
appear	vent
believe	paid

For each box, name the prefix that can be combined correctly with all four words.

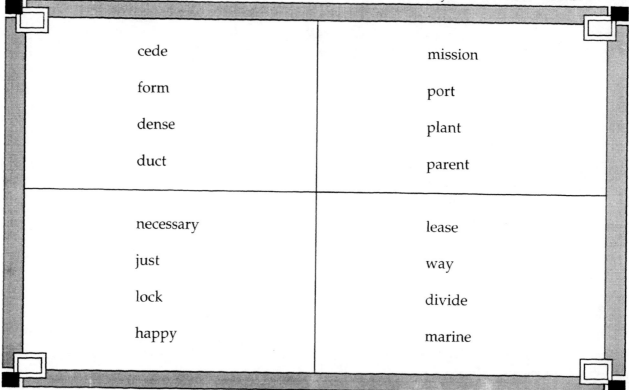

cede	mission
form	port
dense	plant
duct	parent

necessary	lease
just	way
lock	divide
happy	marine

Suffixes

A **suffix** is a letter or sequence of letters that has a specific definition and may be added to the end of a word or base to change its meaning. Pages 33–35 list some common suffixes and a primary definition for each.

Suffix	Definition
-able, -ible	capable or worthy of
-age	action or process; rate of; fee
-ance, -ancy	act, process, or state of being
-ant, -ent	one who performs a specified action
-ate	one who
-cy	state of; position of
-dom	office; state or fact of being
-ence	act, process, or state of being
-er, -or	who or that which does something
-ful	full of; number or quantity that fills

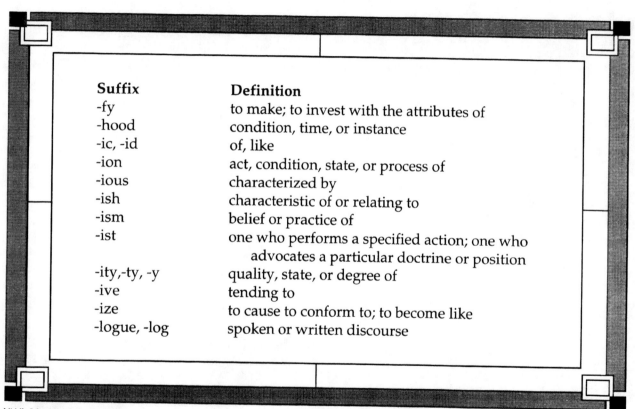

Suffix	Definition
-fy	to make; to invest with the attributes of
-hood	condition, time, or instance
-ic, -id	of, like
-ion	act, condition, state, or process of
-ious	characterized by
-ish	characteristic of or relating to
-ism	belief or practice of
-ist	one who performs a specified action; one who advocates a particular doctrine or position
-ity,-ty, -y	quality, state, or degree of
-ive	tending to
-ize	to cause to conform to; to become like
-logue, -log	spoken or written discourse

Suffix	Definition
-logy	oral or written expression; doctrine, theory, or study of
-ment	act, process, or state of being; concrete result of an action
-ness	state, condition, quality, or degree of
-ory	having the quality of; being characterized by; a place or thing for
-osis	act, condition, or process of
-ous, -ose	full of, having, or possessing the qualities of
-ship	state of being; the art, office, or skill of
-some	causing or characterized by
-tude	state, condition, quality, or degree of
-ward	in the direction of
-y	characterized by, full of, like, or inclined to

Each word in bold ends in a suffix. Choose the best definition for each word.

compulsory
  a. prone to act on impulse
  b. confused, bewildered, or shocked
  c. striking; distinctive
  d. mandatory; enforced

pliable
  a. flexible
  b. oppressive
  c. intact
  d. gullible

foliage
  a. deception
  b. folder for loose papers
  c. leaves on plants and trees
  d. tract of land covered with trees

pernicious
  a. premature
  b. highly destructive or injurious
  c. extremely intelligent
  d. curious; inquisitive

Each word in bold ends in a suffix. Choose the best definition for each word.

verbose
   a. vacant
   b. lush
   c. wordy
   d. practical

lassitude
   a. agitation
   b. a condition of weariness;
      fatigue
   c. a state of mental confusion
   d. bliss

immutable
   a. unable to be heard
   b. incapable of change
   c. capable of being perceived
   d. unavoidable

extemporaneous
   a. unnecessary
   b. experimental
   c. impromptu
   d. extraordinary

Each word in bold ends in a suffix. Choose the best definition for each word.

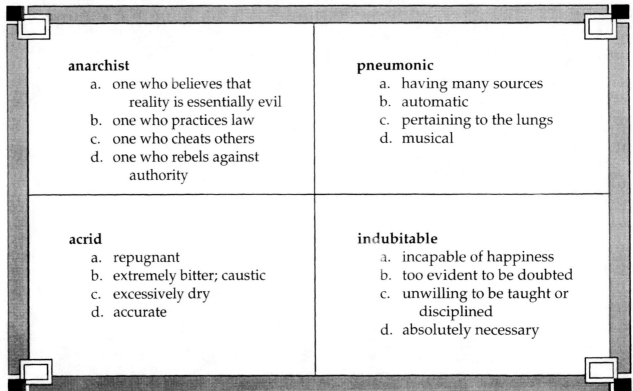

anarchist
- a. one who believes that reality is essentially evil
- b. one who practices law
- c. one who cheats others
- d. one who rebels against authority

pneumonic
- a. having many sources
- b. automatic
- c. pertaining to the lungs
- d. musical

acrid
- a. repugnant
- b. extremely bitter; caustic
- c. excessively dry
- d. accurate

indubitable
- a. incapable of happiness
- b. too evident to be doubted
- c. unwilling to be taught or disciplined
- d. absolutely necessary

Each word in bold ends in a suffix. Choose the best definition for each word.

quiescence
  a. decorative scrollwork
  b. uncertainty
  c. resignation
  d. inactivity; tranquility

brawny
  a. muscular; strong
  b. brainy
  c. shy
  d. harsh; loud

ravenous
  a. pertaining to ravens
  b. jealous
  c. unusually attractive
  d. eager for food, satisfaction, or gratification

vivify
  a. to tell the truth
  b. to give life to; animate
  c. to make empty or vacant
  d. to vigorously protest

Each word in bold ends in a suffix. Choose the best definition for each word.

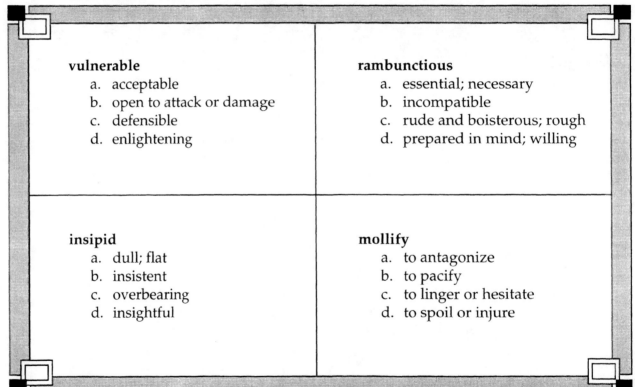

vulnerable
   a. acceptable
   b. open to attack or damage
   c. defensible
   d. enlightening

rambunctious
   a. essential; necessary
   b. incompatible
   c. rude and boisterous; rough
   d. prepared in mind; willing

insipid
   a. dull; flat
   b. insistent
   c. overbearing
   d. insightful

mollify
   a. to antagonize
   b. to pacify
   c. to linger or hesitate
   d. to spoil or injure

For each box, name the suffix that can be combined correctly with all four words.

arm	deal
bash	follow
color	plant
grace	teach

care	avail
friend	depend
home	read
motion	question

Middle School Vocabulary Challenge
© The Learning Works, Inc.

Suffixes

For each box, name the suffix that can be combined correctly with all four words.

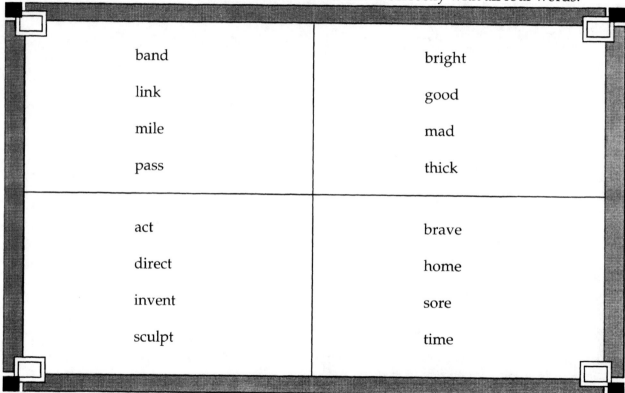

band	bright
link	good
mile	mad
pass	thick
act	brave
direct	home
invent	sore
sculpt	time

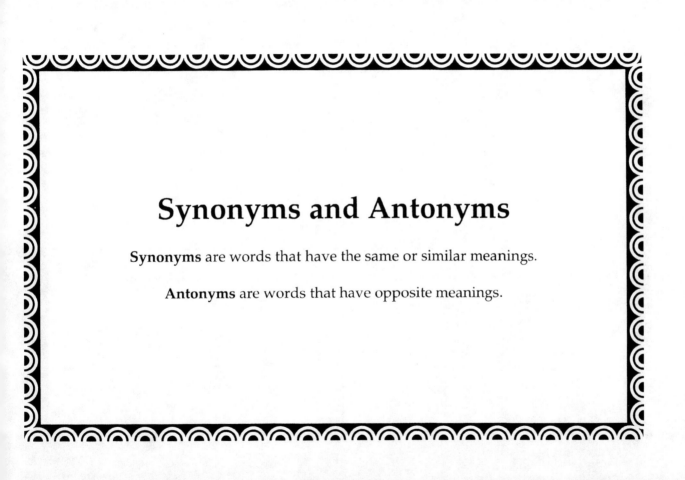

Synonyms and Antonyms

Synonyms are words that have the same or similar meanings.

Antonyms are words that have opposite meanings.

In each group below, find the word that does not belong with the other three synonyms.

optimistic

hopeful

finicky

confident

apprehensive

malicious

spiteful

malevolent

moniker

sobriquet

nickname

caprice

scant

meager

scaly

exiguous

In each group below, find the word that does not belong with the other three synonyms.

indolent

devious

slothful

lazy

fatuous

fallacious

specious

false

scatter

disperse

query

dissipate

paltry

brusque

curt

gruff

In each group below, find the word that does not belong with the other three synonyms.

innuendo

hint

preface

suggestion

quip

quay

jest

joke

lusty

vigorous

energetic

profuse

pinnacle

summit

perigee

apex

In each group below, find the word that does not belong with the other three synonyms.

obstinate	mar
stubborn	petrify
adamant	spoil
abrupt	impair
hasty	entreat
impetuous	beseech
fidgety	implore
sudden	mangle

In each group of words, find the synonym for the word in bold.

alacrity
   a. empathy
   b. abundance
   c. eagerness
   d. sharpness

gregarious
   a. sociable
   b. appreciative
   c. dingy
   d. quarrelsome

languid
   a. jagged
   b. weary
   c. moist
   d. comical

stentorian
   a. elderly
   b. steep
   c. loud
   d. solid

In each group below, find the synonym for the word in bold.

sanctity
   a. health
   b. wisdom
   c. peace
   d. holiness

mediocre
   a. tactless
   b. average
   c. irresponsible
   d. supreme

persevere
   a. persist
   b. prepare
   c. postpone
   d. entangle

vapid
   a. dull
   b. poisonous
   c. consistent
   d. fickle

Middle School Vocabulary Challenge
© The Learning Works, Inc.

Synonyms

In each group below, find the synonym for the word in bold.

append
   a. scold
   b. attach
   c. cancel
   d. neglect

dale
   a. table
   b. shrub
   c. valley
   d. coin

obsequious
   a. proper
   b. servile
   c. glitzy
   d. temporary

lament
   a. aspire
   b. adapt
   c. mourn
   d. scatter

In each group below, find the synonym for the word in bold.

ephemeral
  a. airy
  b. superior
  c. transient
  d. simple

schism
  a. division
  b. angle
  c. journey
  d. outline

proclivity
  a. likeness
  b. fantasy
  c. protector
  d. tendency

unilateral
  a. one-sided
  b. one-legged
  c. alone
  d. single-celled

In each group below, find the synonym for the word in bold.

vacuous
   a. empty
   b. observant
   c. peaceful
   d. fraudulent

knoll
   a. brook
   b. elf
   c. knob
   d. mound

mitigate
   a. guarantee
   b. lessen
   c. rectify
   d. rebel

intractable
   a. prejudiced
   b. slippery
   c. stubborn
   d. honest

In each group below, find the synonym for the word in bold.

betray
- a. inspect
- b. barter
- c. besiege
- d. reveal

stupor
- a. ignorance
- b. insult
- c. lethargy
- d. invasion

haughty
- a. proud
- b. inconsiderate
- c. timid
- d. morbid

staunch
- a. belated
- b. risky
- c. strong
- d. unexplored

In each group below, find the antonym for the word in bold.

ebullient
a. reoccurring
b. learned
c. high-spirited
d. unenthusiastic

vindicate
a. accuse
b. occupy
c. fear
d. defend

synthetic
a. flaky
b. solid
c. natural
d. harmonious

zenith
a. nadir
b. joy
c. enemy
d. interior

In each group below, find the antonym for the word in bold.

antiquated
   a. ancient
   b. modern
   c. offensive
   d. absolute

subservient
   a. domineering
   b. spartan
   c. uplifting
   d. lenient

dissolute
   a. improper
   b. deformed
   c. anxious
   d. moral

radical
   a. negligent
   b. remarkable
   c. conservative
   d. dependable

In each group below, find the antonym for the word in bold.

abate
   a. gain
   b. invent
   c. increase
   d. debit

idle
   a. frigid
   b. busy
   c. intelligent
   d. inadequate

nefarious
   a. conceited
   b. immense
   c. commendable
   d. injurious

repudiate
   a. adopt
   b. repeat
   c. repeal
   d. refuse

In each group below, find the antonym for the word in bold.

fallow
- a. careless
- b. dull
- c. respectful
- d. cultivated

ample
- a. agile
- b. irregular
- c. meager
- d. plenty

loquacious
- a. lonely
- b. sharp
- c. humorous
- d. silent

jovial
- a. melancholy
- b. united
- c. jolly
- d. rude

In each group below, find the antonym for the word in bold.

lithe
   a. inconsiderate
   b. familiar
   c. rigid
   d. dormant

spurn
   a. accept
   b. cleanse
   c. hasten
   d. reject

transparent
   a. terminal
   b. clear
   c. opaque
   d. remove

rescind
   a. withdraw
   b. renew
   c. delay
   d. open

In each group below, find the antonym for the word in bold.

commence
   a. designate
   b. conclude
   c. blunder
   d. regulate

cognizant
   a. formal
   b. visible
   c. popular
   d. ignorant

salubrious
   a. unhealthful
   b. solemn
   c. innovative
   d. defensive

raucous
   a. aloof
   b. calm
   c. melodious
   d. weary

In each group below, find the antonym for the word in bold.

trite
   a. tasty
   b. elastic
   c. original
   d. common

proficiency
   a. servitude
   b. incompetence
   c. preference
   d. obedience

inclement
   a. sharp
   b. mild
   c. alert
   d. steep

colossal
   a. tiny
   b. colonial
   c. close
   d. heavy

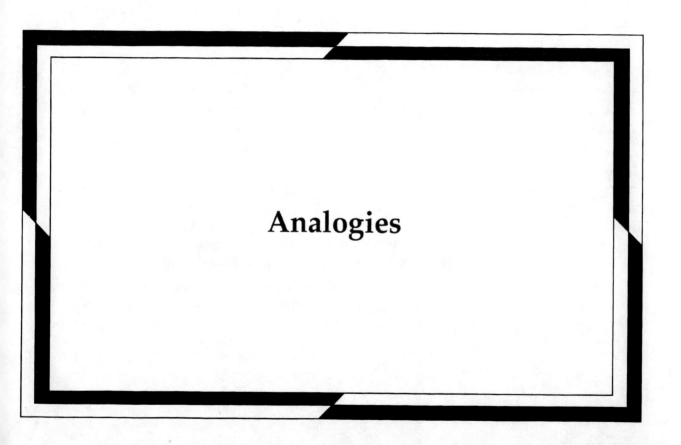

Analogies

What is an Analogy?

An **analogy** is a relationship between one pair of words that serves as the basis for the creation of another pair of words. If the analogy has been completed correctly, the words in the second pair have the same relationship to each other as do the words in the first pair.

What Are These Relationships?

The relationships that form the basis for the completion of analogies vary from one analogy to another. For example, the words in the first pair may be **synonyms**. That is, they may have the same meaning. They may be **antonyms**, terms that have opposite meanings. Or they may be **homophones**, words that have the same sound but have different spellings and different meanings. One term in the pair may name the **group** of which the other term is a **member**. Or one term may name a **whole** of which the other term is a recognized **part**.

No matter what relationship exists between the terms in the first pair, the terms in the second pair must be related to each other in exactly the same way for the analogy to be correct. In other words, if the terms in the first pair are synonyms and the terms in the second pair are antonyms, no analogy exists among the four terms. Their relationship is not **analogous**.

How Do You Write an Analogy?

Analogies are usually written in the form

> <u>gorge</u> is to <u>satiate</u> as <u>conflict</u> is to <u>strife</u>

To shorten this form, a single colon is sometimes used in place of the words *is to*, and a double colon is used in place of the word *as*, to separate the two pairs that make up the analogy.

> gorge : satiate :: conflict : strife

How Do You Complete an Analogy?

Read the first pair of terms and think about the relationship between them. It might help to ask yourself these questions: Are the terms synonyms or antonyms? Are they homophones? Is one a recognized part of the other or a member of the group named by the other?

Example: albatross : bird :: eucalyptus :

- a. fish
- b. flower
- c. leaf
- d. tree

In this example, an <u>albatross</u> is a kind of <u>bird</u>. Thus, <u>bird</u> names the **group** of which <u>albatross</u> is a **member**. What word names the group of which <u>eucalyptus</u> is a member? The word <u>tree</u> correctly completes the analogy.

Sample Analogies

Here are samples of other types of analogies:

Recognized part of a whole
toe : foot :: finger : hand

Individual member of a larger group
reptile : turtle :: bird : swan

An unusual or specific shade of a basic color
azure : blue :: ruby : red

The name given to an animal group
swarm : bees :: covey : quail

The name given to the offspring of a particular animal
cub : bear :: kitten : cat

Tools and the occupations or trades with which they are associated
wrench : plumber :: plow : farmer

Words that name male and female counterparts
gander : goose :: rooster : hen

Choose the word that best completes each analogy.

assume : abdicate :: demean :

a. damper
b. embarrass
c. extol
d. shorten

deception : fraud :: dilemma :

a. faculty
b. sympathy
c. doctrine
d. predicament

ludicrous : ridiculous :: wither :

a. shrivel
b. prudent
c. witty
d. redolent

jurisdiction : power :: decorous :

a. polite
b. rude
c. decorated
d. deceitful

Choose the word that best completes each analogy.

delete : erase :: tenacious :

   a. quiet
   b. vibrant
   c. harsh
   d. persistent

mendacious : dishonest :: sage :

   a. spicy
   b. wise
   c. nervous
   d. neutral

benign : malignant :: laud :

   a. defame
   b. rank
   c. extol
   d. refuse

attractive : repulsive :: obnoxious :

   a. savory
   b. pleasant
   c. gratifying
   d. overbearing

Choose the word that best completes each analogy.

clutch : chicks :: muster :

  a. guns
  b. peacocks
  c. geese
  d. whales

tacit : silent :: chide :

  a. praise
  b. appease
  c. binge
  d. scold

acumen : dullness :: sagacity :

  a. rejection
  b. submissive
  c. foolishness
  d. wisdom

ornithologist : birds :: entomologist :

  a. gems
  b. insects
  c. fishes
  d. reptiles

Choose the word that best completes each analogy.

jaunt : excursion :: lucrative :

a. profitable
b. lingering
c. listless
d. ordinary

sanguine : pessimistic :: stringent :

a. adroit
b. stringy
c. lax
d. meticulous

haughty : arrogant :: impetuous :

a. imminent
b. ignoble
c. haggard
d. impulsive

copious : voluminous :: superfluous :

a. necessary
b. excessive
c. subordinate
d. sublime

Choose the word that best completes each analogy.

abstain : imbibe :: abhor :

- a. cope
- b. hate
- c. approve
- d. advance

confine : enclose :: concoct :

- a. devise
- b. destroy
- c. comfort
- d. conform

masticate : chew :: badger :

- a. dictate
- b. elicit
- c. loathe
- d. annoy

innocuous : harmless :: succinct :

- a. unsavory
- b. copious
- c. concise
- d. verbose

Choose the word that best completes each analogy.

tranquil : calm :: ubiquitous :

    a. eager
    b. adroit
    c. widespread
    d. chivalrous

affect : influence :: somnolent :

    a. affluent
    b. courteous
    c. drowsy
    d. lucid

altruistic : selfish :: vivacious :

    a. prodigious
    b. listless
    c. loquacious
    d. prominent

filbert : nut :: fennel :

    a. herb
    b. fruit
    c. corn
    d. asparagus

Choose the word that best completes each analogy.

anguish : relief :: detrimental :

    a. sympathy
    b. contemporary
    c. fidelity
    d. beneficial

shrink : recoil :: undulate :

    a. untie
    b. regret
    c. swing
    d. isolate

submissive : rebellious :: uncouth :

    a. refined
    b. repugnant
    c. corrupt
    d. official

ibex : mammal :: turbot :

    a. tree
    b. fish
    c. reptile
    d. flower

Choose the word that best completes each analogy.

rooster : chicken :: drake :

   a. hen
   b. bird
   c. ewe
   d. duck

viola : string :: bassoon :

   a. cello
   b. woodwind
   c. orchestra
   d. music

candid : frank :: volition :

   a. choice
   b. violation
   c. honesty
   d. competition

transitory : perpetual :: recalcitrant :

   a. forgetful
   b. unlawful
   c. scrupulous
   d. amenable

Choose the word that best completes each analogy.

affinity : likeness :: aegis :

a. protection
b. enemy
c. atheist
d. affirmation

instigate : incite :: deluge :

a. delve
b. discover
c. inundate
d. deceive

barometer : pressure :: hygrometer :

a. temperature
b. humidity
c. velocity
d. speed

rutabaga : turnip :: casaba :

a. flower
b. vegetable
c. orange
d. melon

Choose the word that best completes each analogy.

aberrant : abnormal :: cajole :

   a. compete
   b. continue
   c. allocate
   d. coax

sabot : feet :: fedora :

   a. head
   b. finger
   c. waist
   d. neck

prominent : inconspicuous :: felicity :

   a. honesty
   b. misery
   c. neglect
   d. trust

pensive : thoughtless :: hirsute :

   a. burdensome
   b. considerate
   c. hesitant
   d. bald

Choose the word that best completes each analogy.

spurious : false :: debacle :

    a. collapse
    b. danger
    c. debate
    d. contempt

kiwi : fruit :: rhea :

    a. reptile
    b. bird
    c. fish
    d. amphibian

weak : decrepit :: venerate :

    a. revere
    b. rattle
    c. vent
    d. deceive

firm : staunch :: austere :

    a. private
    b. wealthy
    c. severe
    d. ominous

Choose the word that best completes each analogy.

obsidian : igneous :: gneiss :

  a. sedimentary
  b. basalt
  c. pebble
  d. metamorphic

impassive : apathetic :: callow :

  a. sophisticated
  b. obstinate
  c. immature
  d. limber

rival : competitor :: umbrage :

  a. umbrella
  b. offense
  c. honor
  d. operation

spin : gyroscope :: oscillate :

  a. fan
  b. motor
  c. bicycle
  d. pendulum

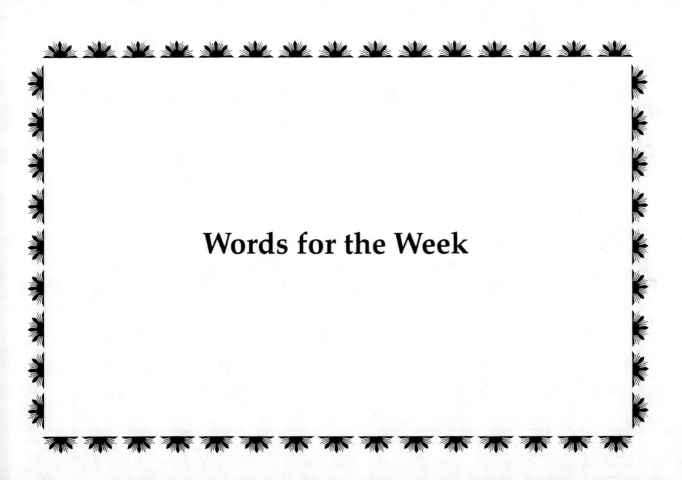

Words for the Week

Words for the Week—Nouns

Match each word with its correct definition.

1. ____ edifice	A. brawl; noisy fight
2. ____ fetish	B. social outcast
3. ____ fracas	C. variety
4. ____ pinnacle	D. building
5. ____ zephyr	E. gentle breeze
6. ____ pariah	F. fixation
7. ____ quandary	G. bell tower
8. ____ mentor	H. coach or tutor
9. ____ diversity	I. peak; summit
10. ____ belfry	J. dilemma; doubt

Words for the Week—Nouns

Match each word with its correct definition.

1. ____ nape
2. ____ candor
3. ____ charlatan
4. ____ ennui
5. ____ paraphernalia
6. ____ dexterity
7. ____ surfeit
8. ____ vendetta
9. ____ gratuity
10. ____ cynic

A. skeptic; pessimist
B. equipment; apparatus
C. frankness; honesty
D. tip for service
E. pretender; quack
F. overabundant supply
G. the back of the neck
H. boredom
I. prolonged feud
J. physical or mental skill

Words for the Week—Nouns

Match each word with its correct definition.

1.	____ penchant	A.	thin covering
2.	____ gripe	B.	descendant
3.	____ misanthrope	C.	complete happiness
4.	____ bliss	D.	poster
5.	____ eulogy	E.	high praise or commendation
6.	____ panacea	F.	complaint; grievance
7.	____ vigil	G.	cure-all
8.	____ scion	H.	a leaning or strong inclination
9.	____ veneer	I.	period of watchful attention
10.	____ placard	J.	one who hates mankind

Words for the Week—Nouns

Match each word with its correct definition.

1. ____ utopia
2. ____ demeanor
3. ____ blitz
4. ____ hierarchy
5. ____ catharsis
6. ____ wrath
7. ____ concordance
8. ____ pedagogue
9. ____ facade
10. ____ guile

A. a purging of the emotions
B. teacher
C. behavior; conduct
D. false or superficial appearance
E. a place of ideal perfection
F. any system of persons or things ranked one above another
G. deceit; cunning
H. a sudden attack
I. anger
J. agreement; harmony

Words for the Week—Nouns

Match each word with its correct definition.

1.	____ pittance	A.	small amount
2.	____ grimace	B.	occupant; holder of an office
3.	____ incumbent	C.	long, heroic story
4.	____ vagrant	D.	talent or aptitude
5.	____ parsimony	E.	stinginess; frugality
6.	____ savvy	F.	look of disgust or disapproval
7.	____ knack	G.	lacking color; paleness
8.	____ nuance	H.	wanderer; rover
9.	____ saga	I.	practical know-how
10.	____ pallor	J.	a subtle quality

Words for the Week—Verbs

Match each word with its correct definition.

1.	____ veer	A.	to refuse to acknowledge
2.	____ juxtapose	B.	to abstain from; avoid
3.	____ condone	C.	assume complete control of
4.	____ ascertain	D.	to change course or direction
5.	____ disavow	E.	to excuse; pardon
6.	____ wane	F.	to expose to loss or danger
7.	____ jeopardize	G.	to send forth
8.	____ monopolize	H.	place side by side for comparison
9.	____ emit	I.	decrease the size, extent, or degree
10.	____ abjure	J.	to find out definitely

Words for the Week—Verbs

Match each word with its correct definition.

1. ____ alleviate	A.	to cause annoyance; enrage
2. ____ propagate	B.	to fill or build up again
3. ____ exploit	C.	to exclude from society
4. ____ ostracize	D.	spread, scatter
5. ____ replenish	E.	lighten, make easier
6. ____ affirm	F.	to examine in detail; study
7. ____ peruse	G.	multiply; produce
8. ____ maim	H.	to take advantage of; profit by
9. ____ disseminate	I.	to wound seriously; disable
10. ____ exasperate	J.	to state positively; validate

Words for the Week—Verbs

Match each word with its correct definition.

1. ____ discriminate
2. ____ merge
3. ____ emulate
4. ____ promulgate
5. ____ deter
6. ____ interrogate
7. ____ scintillate
8. ____ evict
9. ____ fluctuate
10. ____ dissipate

A. to scatter
B. to make known; proclaim
C. to strive to equal or excel
D. to sparkle
E. to distinguish between
F. to force out; expel
G. mix or blend
H. to discourage; inhibit
I. to alternate; shift
J. to question

Words for the Week—Verbs

Match each word with its correct definition.

1. ____ intone
2. ____ oblige
3. ____ gnash
4. ____ ruminate
5. ____ seclude
6. ____ encompass
7. ____ intervene
8. ____ flaunt
9. ____ transgress
10. ____ feign

A. utter or recite in monotone
B. to surround
C. to parade or display conspicuously
D. to go beyond the limit or boundaries
E. grind or strike the teeth together
F. make a false show of
G. to place under a debt of gratitude for some service or favor
H. to chew a cud; to ponder at length
I. to come between
J. isolate

Words for the Week—Adjectives

Match each word with its correct definition.

1. ____ exuberant
2. ____ tantamount
3. ____ benevolent
4. ____ inaudible
5. ____ disheveled
6. ____ obtuse
7. ____ parched
8. ____ catastrophic
9. ____ congenial
10. ____ senile

A. equivalent in value or effect
B. disorderly; untidy
C. marked by a decline of mental faculties associated with old age
D. incapable of being heard
E. dry
F. agreeable
G. insensitive; dull
H. disastrous
I. charitable; kindly
J. full of high spirits

Words for the Week—Adjectives

Match each word with its correct definition.

1. ____ lugubrious
2. ____ curt
3. ____ compatible
4. ____ infinitesimal
5. ____ gawky
6. ____ feckless
7. ____ indigenous
8. ____ covert
9. ____ obese
10. ____ strident

A. exaggeratedly or affectedly mournful
B. unthinking; irresponsible
C. excessively overweight
D. secret
E. immeasurably small
F. rudely brief in speech; abrupt in manner
G. well-matched
H. native
I. clumsy; awkward
J. shrill; harsh

Words for the Week—Adjectives

Match each word with its correct definition.

1. ____ adamant
2. ____ malleable
3. ____ conspicuous
4. ____ inanimate
5. ____ notorious
6. ____ cagey
7. ____ squeamish
8. ____ indolent
9. ____ capricious
10. ____ fervent

A. impulsive; whimsical
B. inclined to become nauseated
C. lifeless
D. lazy
E. impassioned
F. having a widely known and usually bad reputation
G. noticeable
H. wary
I. capable of being formed or shaped
J. unyielding

Words for the Week—Adjectives

Match each word with its correct definition.

1. ____ nebulous
2. ____ effulgent
3. ____ quixotic
4. ____ brusque
5. ____ erudite
6. ____ banal
7. ____ lurid
8. ____ impudent
9. ____ conducive
10. ____ irascible

A. shining forth brilliantly; radiant
B. gruesome; shocking
C. blunt; abrupt
D. lacking originality; hackneyed
E. marked by rude boldness or disrespect
F. scholarly; knowledgeable
G. easily provoked to anger
H. vague; not clear
I. extravagantly chivalrous or romantic; impractical
J. helpful

Fun With Words

Tricky Words

Match each tricky word with its correct definition.

1. ____ accede (verb)   A. to bring about
2. ____ exceed (verb)   B. to surpass
3. ____ accept (verb)   C. to influence
4. ____ except (verb)   D. expert; skillful; proficient
5. ____ adapt (verb)   E. to leave out
6. ____ adept (adjective)   F. the result
7. ____ adopt (verb)   G. to assume an office or position
8. ____ affect (verb)   H. to receive as one's own
9. ____ effect (verb)   I. to receive
10. ____ effect (noun)   J. to change or adjust

Tricky Words

Match each tricky word with its correct definition.

1. ____ allude (verb)   A. agreement or approval

2. ____ elude (verb)   B. a reference

3. ____ allusion (noun)   C. a completing part

4. ____ illusion (noun)   D. to draw forth or bring about

5. ____ ascent (noun)   E. the act of climbing or going up

6. ____ assent (noun)   F. an expression of admiration

7. ____ complement (noun)   G. not permitted; unlawful

8. ____ compliment (noun)   H. to dodge or slip away from

9. ____ elicit (verb)   I. to make brief or vague reference

10. ____ illicit (adjective)   J. something that deceives, misleads, or
                                   plays tricks upon

Tricky Words

Match each tricky word with its correct definition.

1. ____ emigrate (verb)
2. ____ immigrate (verb)
3. ____ assay (verb)
4. ____ essay (verb)
5. ____ consul (noun)
6. ____ council (noun)
7. ____ counsel (noun)
8. ____ conscience (noun)
9. ____ conscientious (adjective)
10. ____ conscious (adjective)

A. a sense of right
B. a government representative
C. to leave one's own country for another
D. having rational power
E. to analyze or test
F. to come into a country of which one is not a native for permanent residence
G. governed by conscience; meticulous
H. to attempt
I. an assembly of persons convened for deliberation
J. advice

Tricky Words

Match each tricky word with its correct definition.

1. _____ persecute (verb)
2. _____ prosecute (verb)
3. _____ precede (verb)
4. _____ proceed (verb)
5. _____ decent (adjective)
6. _____ descent (noun)
7. _____ dissent (noun)
8. _____ principal (adjective)
9. _____ principal (noun)
10. _____ principle (noun)

A. to be, come, or go ahead or in front of
B. conforming to standards of propriety, good taste, or morality
C. most important
D. difference of opinion; disagreement
E. a general or fundamental truth
F. to oppress or harass
G. to initiate criminal action against
H. the act of going from a higher to a lower level
I. to continue after a pause
J. a chief or head woman or man

Odd Word Out

In each group of words, all the words have something in common except one.
Find the odd word and write the reason why it doesn't belong.

garnish	clavier
mince	chisel
eradicate	sitar
blanch	zither
truss	ocarina
saris	hora
espadrilles	tarantella
thongs	gavotte
clogs	rigadoon
sabots	guilder

Odd Word Out

In each group of words, all the words have something in common except one.
Find the odd word and write the reason why it doesn't belong.

cravat	bushel
creel	hertz
bolero	joule
ascot	rune
mackinaw	watt
myna	fedora
tern	bunco
petrel	tiara
marabou	derby
vassal	beret

Itises

Words ending in -itis usually name an inflammation.
Tell what part of the body is inflamed for each -itis below.

arthritis	gingivitis
hepatitis	phlebitis

Itises

Words ending in -itis usually name an inflammation.
Tell what part of the body is inflamed for each -itis below.

pericarditis	osteomyelitis
neuritis	ophthalmitis

Phobias

A phobia is an intense, abnormal, or unreasonable fear of a particular type of person, place, thing, or situation. Tell what a person would fear for each phobia below.

claustrophobia	nyctophobia
hemophobia	agoraphobia

Phobias

A phobia is an intense, abnormal, or unreasonable fear of a particular type of person, place, thing, or situation. Tell what a person would fear for each phobia below.

pyrophobia	acrophobia
entomophobia	hypnophobia

Food Words

Describe the food you would be eating for each term below.

hasenpfeffer	escargot
succotash	vichyssoise

Food Words

Describe the food you would be eating for each term below.

damson	filbert
pippin	kohlrabi

Anagrams

An anagram is a word created by rearranging the letters of another word without adding or subtracting any letters.

Example: horse = shore

Write an anagram for each word below.

throw	secure
master	drapes

Anagrams

An anagram is a word created by rearranging the letters of another word without adding or subtracting any letters.

Example: horse = shore

Write an anagram for each word below.

notices	crate
thing	danger

Mystery Words

All four words in each group can be paired with a fifth word to form a compound word.

Example:	
man lift high wheel	The mystery word is *chair*: chairman, chairlift, highchair, wheelchair

Write the word that goes before or after each word in the sets below.

pass wear mine stand	time size boat jacket
locked mark scape lady	less book dead paper

Mystery Words

All four words in each group can be paired with a fifth word to form a compound word.

Example:	
man lift high wheel	The mystery word is *chair*: chairman, chairlift, highchair, wheelchair

Write the word that goes before or after each word in the sets below.

horn life shot be	back work boy weight
case mark note end	ship die ware boiled

Occupations and Hobbies

Each word below is the name of a specific area of study.
Name the occupation or hobby each word describes.

paleontology	herpetology
podiatry	genealogy

Occupations and Hobbies

Each word below is the name of a specific area of study.
Name the occupation or hobby each word describes.

ornithology	pathology
graphology	philology

Occupations and Hobbies

Each word below is the name of a specific area of study.
Name the occupation or hobby each word describes.

etymology	ichthyology
endocrinology	botany

Occupations and Hobbies

Each word below is the name of a specific area of study.
Name the occupation or hobby each word describes.

geology	cardiology
dermatology	agronomy

Name That Color

Name the color that each word describes.

ecru	alabaster
cinnabar	slate
ocher	taupe
azure	xanthic
umber	vermilion
malachite	ultramarine
dun	saffron
carmine	sorrel

Words From Mythology

The following words in bold are all derived from mythology.
Circle the letter of the best definition for each word in bold.

nemesis
- a. a fictitious name
- b. an elaborate banquet
- c. a powerful opponent
- d. a demand or request

herculean
- a. extremely strong
- b. a strong belief
- c. a dangerous situation
- d. weightless

odyssey
- a. an unusual occurrence
- b. a threat
- c. a spiritual journey
- d. an attack

lethargic
- a. illiterate
- b. indifferent; lazy; listless
- c. according to the law
- d. clear-cut

Animal Groups

Fill in the name of the animal group for each animal listed below.

Example: a *pack* of dogs

a _____ of larks or quails

a _____ of bees

a _____ of peacocks

a _____ of coots

a _____ of foxes

a _____ of geese

a _____ of kangaroos or monkeys

a _____ of bears

a _____ of turkeys

a _____ of birds

a _____ of pheasants

a _____ of seals or whales

a _____ of sheep or pigs

a _____ of chicks

a _____ of badgers

a _____ of mallards

Animal Offspring

Write the name of the offspring of each animal below.
(Answers may be used more than once.) **Example:** bear *cub*

a. giraffe
b. zebra
c. turkey
d. deer

a. goose
b. whale
c. oyster
d. eel

a. ostrich
b. kangaroo
c. goat
d. hawk

a. otter
b. fish
c. eagle
d. duck

Animal Words

Each word below is associated with animals.
Write the word that best completes each phrase.

simian—having to do with
   a. insects or spiders
   b. birds
   c. monkeys or apes
   d. reptiles

apiary—having to do with
   a. bees
   b. birds
   c. cats
   d. pigs

bovine—having to do with
   a. boll weevils
   b. horses
   c. foxes
   d. cows and oxen

feline—having to do with
   a. cats
   b. fishes
   c. eagles
   d. deer

Bird, Fish, or Mammal?

Decide if each word below names a bird, fish, or mammal.
(Use a dictionary if you need help.)

a. adjutant
b. wombat
c. shad
d. civet

a. capybara
b. markhor
c. kea
d. discus

a. okapi
b. coati
c. grunt
d. bonito

a. kestrel
b. tanager
c. hake
d. galago

Cat Words

Each word in bold begins with the word cat.
Select the best definition for each *cat* word.

catapult
   a. to exchange foreign currency
   b. to launch by means of a device
      utilizing a spring
   c. to possess or control
   d. to stir up or excite

catacomb
   a. wide-toothed comb
   b. community center
   c. formal speech or statement
   d. subterranean cemetery

catatonic
   a. mentally keen or quick
   b. having to do with sound
   c. in a state of stupor
   d. a style of music

catamaran
   a. harbor
   b. instrument used to measure
      distance
   c. boat with two parallel hulls
   d. outer room of a building

Dog Words

Each word in bold begins with the word dog.
Select the best definition for each *dog* word.

dogma

  a. praise
  b. boundary
  c. emblem or symbol
  d. doctrine; belief

dogmatic

  a. arrogant in stating an opinion
  b. heavily populated
  c. critical
  d. automatic

dogged

  a. friendly
  b. persistent; stubborn
  c. unhappy, sad
  d. ragged

dogwood

  a. musical instrument with strings
  b. small tree bearing white or pink flowers
  c. colorless, odorless liquid
  d. small game bird with short legs

Word List

A

abate, 56
abdicate, 26
abhor, 69
abjure, 83
abrade, 26
abrupt, 47
abscond, 26
absolve, 26
accede, 92
accept, 92
acrid, 38
acrimonious, 15
acrophobia, 101
adamant, 89
adapt, 92
adept, 92
adjutant, 117

adopt, 92
adroit, 10
aegis, 73
affect, 92
affirm, 84
agitate, 19
agoraphobia, 100
agronomy, 111
alabaster, 112
alacrity, 48
alleviate, 84
allude, 93
allusion, 93
ample, 57
anarchist, 38
antiquated, 55
apiary, 116
append, 50

apprehensive, 44
arthritis, 98
ascent, 93
ascertain, 83
assay, 94
assent, 93
assimilate, 8
astute, 14
austere, 75
azure, 112

B

badger, 69
banal, 90
bassoon, 72
belfry, 78
benevolent, 87
betray, 53

bliss, 80
blitz, 81
bonito, 117
botany, 110
bovine, 116
brawny, 39
brusque, 90
buffoon, 24
bunco, 97

C

cagey, 89
cajole, 74
callow, 76
candor, 79
capitulate, 17
caprice, 44
capricious, 89

Word List

capybara, 117
cardiology, 111
carmine, 112
casaba, 73
catacomb, 118
catamaran, 118
catapult, 118
catastrophic, 87
catatonic, 118
catharsis, 81
charlatan, 79
chide, 67
chisel, 96
cinnabar, 112
circumference, 28
circumlunar, 28
circumnavigate, 28
circumscribe, 28

civet, 117
claustrophobia, 100
coati, 117
cognizant, 59
colossal, 60
commence, 59
compatible, 88
complement, 93
compliment, 93
compulsory, 36
concede, 14
concise, 10
concoct, 69
concordance, 81
condone, 83
conducive, 90
congenial, 87
conscience, 94

conscientious, 94
conscious, 94
conspicuous, 89
consul, 94
contraband, 26
contradict, 26
contrive, 24
controversy, 26
cordial, 20
council, 94
counsel, 94
countermand, 26
covert, 88
credence, 19
creel, 97
curt, 88
cynic, 79

D

dale, 50
damson, 103
dearth, 21
debacle, 75
decent, 95
decorous, 65
deluge, 73
demean, 65
demeanor, 81
dermatology, 111
descent, 95
deter, 85
detrimental, 71
devious, 45
dexterity, 79
dilemma, 65
disavow, 83

Word List

discriminate, 85
discus, 117
disheveled, 87
disperse, 17
disseminate, 84
dissent, 95
dissipate, 85
dissolute, 55
diversity, 78
divulge, 15
docile, 21
dogged, 119
dogma, 119
dogmatic, 119
dogwood, 119
domicile, 23
dormant, 22
dowdy, 18

drake, 72
dubious, 16
dun, 112

E
ebullient, 54
ecru, 112
edifice, 78
effect, 92
effulgent, 90
elicit, 93
elude, 93
emigrate, 94
emit, 83
emulate, 85
encompass, 86
endocrinology, 110
ennui, 79

entomologist, 67
entomophobia, 101
ephemeral, 51
erudite, 90
eradicate, 96
escargot, 102
eschew, 22
essay, 94
etymology, 110
eulogy, 80
evict, 85
exasperate, 84
exceed, 92
except, 92
exploit, 84
extemporaneous, 37
exuberant, 87

F
facade, 81
facetious, 10
fallow, 57
fatuous, 45
feasible, 24
feckless, 88
fedora, 74
feign, 86
felicity, 74
feline, 116
fennel, 70
fervent, 89
fetish, 78
fiasco, 10
fidgety, 47
filbert, 103
finicky, 44

Word List

flamboyant, 17
flaunt, 86
fluctuate, 85
foliage, 36
fortitude, 9
fracas, 78
frivolous, 14
frugal, 15

G
galago, 117
gamut, 16
garish, 23
gawky, 88
genealogy, 108
geology, 111
gingivitis, 98
gnash, 86

gneiss, 76
graphology, 109
gratuity, 79
gregarious, 48
grimace, 82
gripe, 80
grunt, 117
guilder, 96
guile, 81

H
hake, 117
hasenpfeffer, 102
haughty, 53
hemophobia, 100
hepatitis, 98
herculean, 113
herpetology, 108

hierarchy, 81
hirsute, 74
hygrometer, 73
hyperbole, 26
hyperpnea, 26
hyperpyrexia, 26
hypertension, 26
hypnophobia, 101
hypodermic, 27
hypogenous, 27
hypopnea, 27
hypothermia, 27

I
ichthyology, 110
idle, 56
illicit, 93
illusion, 93

immigrate, 94
immutable, 37
impede, 8
impetuous, 68
impudent, 90
inanimate, 89
inaudible, 87
inclement, 60
incumbent, 82
indigenous, 88
indolent, 89
indubitable, 38
infinitesimal, 88
insipid, 40
intercede, 27
intercoastal, 27
intermittent, 27
interpret, 27

Word List

interrogate, 85
intervene, 86
intone, 86
intractable, 52
irascible, 90

J
jaunt, 18
jeopardize, 83
jovial, 57
juxtapose, 83

K
kea, 117
kestrel, 117
knack, 82
knoll, 52
kohlrabi, 103

L
lament, 50
languid, 48
lassitude, 37
laud, 66
lethargic, 113
lithe, 58
loiter, 18
loquacious, 57
lucrative, 68
ludicrous, 20

lugubrious, 88
lurid, 90

M
magnanimous, 13
maim, 84
malachite, 112
maladroit, 27
malaise, 27
malfunction, 27
malign, 27
malleable, 89
mangle, 47
marabou, 97
markhor, 117
mediocre, 49
mentor, 78
merge, 85

mettle, 11
misanthrope, 80
mitigate, 52
mollify, 40
monocle, 28
monologue, 28
monopolize, 83
monopoly, 28
monotonous, 28
muster, 67

N
nape, 79
nebulous, 90
nefarious, 56
nemesis, 113
neuritis, 99
notorious, 89

Word List

novice, 11
nuance, 82
nyctophobia, 100

O

obese, 88
obfuscate, 19
oblige, 86
obliterate, 13
obnoxious, 66
obsequious, 50
obtuse, 87
ocher, 112
odyssey, 113
okapi, 117
omnifarious, 26
omnipotent, 26
omniscient, 26

omnivorous, 26
ophthalmitis, 99
opulent, 16
ornithology, 109
oscillate, 76
osteomyelitis, 99
ostracize, 84

P

pacify, 13
paleontology, 108
pallor, 82
paltry, 45
panacea, 80
paradox, 9
paraphernalia, 79
parched, 87
pariah, 78

parsimony, 82
pathology, 109
pedagogue, 81
penchant, 80
pericarditis, 99
perigee, 46
periphery, 22
pernicious, 36
persecute, 95
persevere, 49
peruse, 84
petrify, 47
philology, 109
phlebitis, 98
pilfer, 23
pinnacle, 78
pippin, 103
pittance, 82

placard, 80
plethora, 11
pliable, 36
plutocracy, 21
pneumonic, 38
podiatry, 108
posthumous, 18
postmortem, 28
postoperative, 28
postpone, 28
postscript, 28
precede, 95
precipice, 12
preface, 46
principal, 95
principle, 95
proceed, 95
proclivity, 51

Word List

proficiency, 60
profuse, 46
promulgate, 85
propagate, 84
prosecute, 95
pyrophobia, 100

Q

quadrant, 27
quadrennial, 27
quadrille, 27
quadruplet, 27
quandary, 78
quay, 46
query, 45
quiescence, 39
quixotic, 90

R

radical, 55
rambunctious, 40
rancid, 9
raucous, 59
ravenous, 39
recalcitrant, 72
redolent, 16
replenish, 84
replicate, 20
reprimand, 11
repudiate, 56
rescind, 58
rhea, 75
ruminate, 86
rune, 97

S

saffron, 112
saga, 82
sagacity, 67
sage, 66
salient, 22
salubrious, 59
sanctity, 49
saris, 96
savvy, 82
scaly, 44
schism, 51
scintillate, 85
scion, 80
seclude, 86
senile, 87
shad, 117
simian, 116

slate, 112
somnolent, 70
sorrel, 112
sporadic, 24
spurn, 58
squeamish, 89
staunch, 53
stentorian, 48
strident, 88
stringent, 68
stupor, 53
subservient, 55
succinct, 69
succotash, 102
superfluous, 68
surfeit, 79
synthetic, 54

Word List

T

tanager, 117
tantamount, 87
taupe, 112
tawdry, 20
tenacious, 66
tenuous, 23
thwart, 15
transgress, 86
transitory, 9
transparent, 58
travesty, 21
treacherous, 12
trepidation, 13
trident, 28
trilogy, 28
tripod, 28
trisect, 28

trite, 60
tumult, 14
turbot, 71

U

ubiquitous, 70
ultramarine, 112
umber, 112
umbrage, 76
uncouth, 71
undulate, 71
unilateral, 51
urbane, 8
usurp, 8
utopia, 81

V

vacuous, 52
vagrant, 82
validate, 12
vapid, 49
vassal, 97
veer, 83
vendetta, 79
veneer, 80
venerate, 75
verbose, 37
vermilion, 112
vichyssoise, 102
vigil, 80
vindicate, 54
vivacious, 70
vivify, 39
volatile, 17

volition, 72
voracious, 19
vulnerable, 40

W

wane, 83
wither, 65
wizened, 12
wombat, 117
wrath, 81

X

xanthic, 112

Z

zenith, 54
zephyr, 78

Answer Key

Page 8
d
a
c
a

Page 9
b
c
a
b

Page 10
e
a
b
e

Page 11
b
b
d
a

Page 12
a
a
c
e

Page 13
c
e
c
a

Page 14
b
d
e
b

Page 15
c
b
c
d

Page 16
e
c
d
a

Page 17
b
a
d
c

Page 18
e
a
b
c

Page 19
c
a
e
c

Page 20
d
a
b
a

Page 21
b
e
b
e

Page 22
c
d
c
b

Page 23
c
a
d
e

Page 24
e
b
c
a

Answer Key

Page 26

disinherit; renounce
scrape away
escape
forgive; pardon

oppose
illegal smuggled goods
a dispute
to revoke or reverse

very high fever
an exaggeration or overstatement
high blood pressure
unusually rapid breathing

unlimited in power or authority
feeding on both animal and vegetable substances
knowing all things; extensive knowledge
of all kinds or varieties

Page 27

mediate; intervene
extending between seacoasts
translate; to explain the meaning of
coming and going at intervals; not continuous

a vague discomfort often at the onset of illness
unskillful; awkward; bungling
to speak evil of
the failure to work

a quarter section of a circle
a square dance performed by four couples
a group of four; one of four offspring born at one birth
lasting four years, occurring once every four years

low body temperature
shallow breathing
underground; growing on the underside of
of or pertaining to the area under the skin

Answer Key

Page 28
a three-pronged spear
a set of three related plays, novels, etc.
a three-legged stool, table, pedestal, or stand
to cut into three equal parts

to put off; to defer to a later time
an autopsy; the examination of a body after death
a short message added at the end of a letter
following surgery

a speech by one person
exclusive ownership
lacking variety
an eyeglass for one eye

to go completely around
to draw a line around
the perimeter of a circle
revolving around the moon

Page 29
ex-
pro-
de-
in-

Page 30
com-
mis-
per-
non-

Page 31
im-
re-
dis-
pre-

Page 32
con-
trans-
un-
sub-

Page 36
d
a
c
b

Page 37
c
b
b
c

Page 38
d
c
b
b

Page 41
-ful
-er
-less
-able

Page 42
-age
-ness
-or
-ly

Answer Key

Page 39
d
a
d
b

Page 40
b
c
a
b

Page 44
finicky
apprehensive
caprice
scaly

Page 45
devious
fatuous
query
paltry

Page 46
preface
quay
profuse
perigee

Page 47
abrupt
petrify
fidgety
mangle

Page 48
c
a
b
c

Page 49
d
b
a
a

Page 50
b
c
b
c

Page 51
c
a
d
a

Page 52
a
d
b
c

Page 53
d
c
a
c

Page 54
d
a
c
a

Page 55
b
a
d
c

Page 56
c
b
c
a

Page 57
d
c
d
a

Page 58
c
a
c
b

Page 59
b
d
a
c

Page 60
c
b
b
a

Page 65
c
d
a
a

Answer Key

Page 66
d
b
a
b

Page 67
b
d
c
b

Page 68
a
c
d
b

Page 69
c
a
d
c

Page 70
c
c
b
a

Page 71
d
c
a
b

Page 72
d
b
a
d

Page 73
a
c
b
d

Page 74
d
a
b
d

Page 75
a
b
a
c

Page 76
d
c
b
d

Page 78
1. D
2. F
3. A
4. I
5. E
6. B
7. J
8. H
9. C
10. G

Page 79
1. G
2. C
3. E
4. H
5. B
6. J
7. F
8. I
9. D
10. A

Page 80
1. H
2. F
3. J
4. C
5. E
6. G
7. I
8. B
9. A
10. D

Page 81
1. E
2. C
3. H
4. F
5. A
6. I
7. J
8. B
9. D
10. G

Answer Key

Page 82
1. A
2. F
3. B
4. H
5. E
6. I
7. D
8. J
9. C
10. G

Page 83
1. D
2. H
3. E
4. J
5. A
6. I
7. F
8. C
9. G
10. B

Page 84
1. E
2. G
3. H
4. C
5. B
6. J
7. F
8. I
9. D
10. A

Page 85
1. E
2. G
3. C
4. B
5. H
6. J
7. D
8. F
9. I
10. A

Page 86
1. A
2. G
3. E
4. H
5. J
6. B
7. I
8. C
9. D
10. F

Page 87
1. J
2. A
3. I
4. D
5. B
6. G
7. E
8. H
9. F
10. C

Page 88
1. A
2. F
3. G
4. E
5. I
6. B
7. H
8. D
9. C
10. J

Page 89
1. J
2. I
3. G
4. C
5. F
6. H
7. B
8. D
9. A
10. E

Page 90
1. H
2. A
3. I
4. C
5. F
6. D
7. B
8. E
9. J
10. G

Page 92
1. G
2. B
3. I
4. E
5. J
6. D
7. H
8. C
9. A
10. F

Answer Key

Page 93
1. I
2. H
3. B
4. J
5. E
6. A
7. C
8. F
9. D
10. G

Page 94
1. C
2. F
3. E
4. H
5. B
6. I
7. J
8. A
9. G
10. D

Page 95
1. F
2. G
3. A
4. I
5. B
6. H
7. D
8. C
9. J
10. E

Page 96
vocalize (not something you do to food)
chisel (not a musical instrument)
saris (not something worn on the feet)
guilder (not a dance)

Page 97
creel (not something you wear)
rune (not a unit of measure)
vassal (not a type of bird)
bunco (not something worn on the head)

Page 98
joint
gums
liver
vein

Page 99
pericardium or tissue covering the heart
bone or marrow
nerve
eye

Answer Key

Page 100
narrow or closed places
night, darkness
blood
open spaces

Page 101
flames or fire
heights
insects
sleep

Page 102
rabbit stew
snail
a mixture of corn and beans
a cold soup made of leeks or onions and
    potatoes

Page 103
plum
nut
apple
cabbage

Page 104
(answers may vary)
worth
rescue
stream
spread

Page 105
(answers may vary)
section
react
night
garden

Page 106
under
life
land
end

Page 107
long
paper
book
hard

Page 108
fossils
amphibians and reptiles
feet
families and ancestors

Page 109
birds
diseased tissues
handwriting
literature or linguistics

Page 110
word origins and histories
fishes
glands
plants

Page 111
rocks
hearts
skin
soil

Answer Key

Page 112
tan
red
yellow
blue

white
gray
gray
yellow

brown
green
brown
red; purplish-red

red
blue
yellow
brown

Page 113
c
a
c
b

Page 114
bevy
hive
muster
covert

skulk
gaggle
troop
sloth

rafter
brood
nide
pod

drove
clutch
cete
sord

Page 115
calf
colt
poult
fawn

gosling
calf
spat
leptocephalus

chick
joey
kid
eyas

whelp
fry
eaglet
duckling

Page 116
c. monkeys or apes
a. bees
d. cows and oxen
a. cats

Page 117
a. bird
b. mammal
c. fish
d. mammal

a. mammal
b. mammal
c. bird
d. fish

a. mammal
b. bird
c. fish
d. fish

a. bird
b. bird
c. fish
d. mammal

Page 118
b
d
c
c

Page 119
d
a
b
b